A **FALCON** GUIDE®

B A S I C   E S S E N T I A L S ®   S E R I E S

BASIC ESSENTIALS®
Bicycle
Touring

Second Edition

DENNIS STUHAUG

FALCON GUIDE®

GUILFORD, CONNECTICUT
HELENA, MONTANA
AN IMPRINT OF THE GLOBE PEQUOT PRESS

A FALCON GUIDE ®

Text and layout design by Nancy Freeborn

Photo on page 3 by Juliet Fisher; chapter opener spot photos © Clipart.com; all other photos and illustrations by Dennis Stuhaug.

Library of Congress Cataloging-in-Publication Data
Stuhaug, Dennis O.
  Basic essentials. Bicycle touring / Dennis Stuhaug. — 2nd ed.
    p. cm. — (Basic essentials series)
  ISBN-13: 978-0-7627-4009-3
  ISBN-10: 0-7627-4009-4
  1. Bicycle touring. I. Title.
  GV1044.S78 2006
  796.6'4—dc22   2006026126

To buy books in quantity for corporate use or incentives, call **(800) 962–0973, ext. 4551,** or e-mail **premiums@GlobePequot.com.**

We courted on bikes, we rode to work on our bikes, we vacationed on our bikes, we headed to the park for a family picnic on our bikes. We learned, along the way, how to ride in and on a tandem. This book is for Suzanne, with whom the ride tomorrow will be the best yet.

Help Us Keep This Guide Up to Date

Every effort has been made by the editors to make this guide as accurate and useful as possible. However, many things can change after a guide is published—establishments close, phone numbers change, methods and techniques evolve, equipement changes, etc.

We would love to hear from you concerning your experiences with this guide and how you feel it could be improved and kept up to date. While we may not be able to respond to all comments and suggestions, we'll take them to heart and we'll also make certain to share them with the editors. Please send your comments and suggestions to the following address:

The Globe Pequot Press
Reader Response/Editorial Department
P.O. Box 480
Guilford, CT 06437

Or you may e-mail us at:

editorial@GlobePequot.com

Thanks for your input, and happy travels!

Contents

Acknowledgments

I've had the great good fortune to ride with some splendid cyclists, and attempting to recognize them all would make this a much longer book. I owe a great debt of gratitude to Jerry Baker, racer, rider, manufacturer, and ceaseless promoter—and a pleasure to ride with. Ken Green rode with a fantastic sense of humor and fierce drive. Others who have shaped how I ride include the Cohen family of West Coast Cycle (Nishiki, now part of Derby Cycle), Alan and Hanz Scholz of Green Gear Cycle, Dave Levy of Ti Cycles, Bob Forman and Bill Davidson of Elliott Bay Cycles, the folks at Burley Design Cooperative, cyclists and writers Jim Langley (www.jimlangley.com) and Fred Matheny (www.Road BikeRider.com), and Glenn Erickson as a framebuilder, racer, and rider. Lon Haldeman shared his passion for cycling. This book could not have happened without the patience, skill, and good graces of editors Bill Schneider and Mike Urban at FalconGuides/Globe Pequot Press and their editing and design team.

We once found ourselves on the wrong side of the small Italian town of Montebelluna just as the evening commuters poured out onto the narrow street. Riding through would have severely challenged our traffic skills, and pedaling around would've meant a long, arduous series of climbs at the end of a stiff day. We waved to a car and pointed at ourselves and the driver's rear fender. He gave us a big smile and a nod. I held my hands up a few inches apart, asking if we could closely draft behind him. He nodded, then asked where we were headed. We told him the name of the agri-tourist inn on the far side of the town. When the light changed, we followed him into the snarl of traffic at 40 to 50 kilometers per hour. (it was downhill at first). We sailed behind him from one side of town to the other, and he soon pulled into the small road we would have to climb to our inn. "Thank you very much," my wife and stoker called to the policeman and his partner in the car.

"Good ride, good ride," they replied.

And it has been.

Introduction

Why Do We Ride?

Each year on a Saturday in early July about 9,000 people clamber aboard their bikes in Seattle, Washington, and pedal off over 200 miles of rural roads and byways to Portland, Oregon.

About 7,000 pull off the road at the halfway point to eat dinner, swap stories, and head off for well-deserved rest. They camp in tents and RVs, stay in motels, or spread out in gymnasiums and church halls. On Sunday morning they meet for breakfast and push on—perhaps stiffly—for the second hundred miles to the finish line.

The remaining 2,000 riders use the halfway mark as an early lunch spot, a restroom break, and a place to replace flatted tubes or regroup with friends. After twenty minutes or so they are back on the road, heading for a late afternoon or early evening arrival in Portland. The larger group is on a bicycle tour; the smaller one is on a bike ride.

On that same weekend, groups of touring cyclists will be riding 20 miles a day as they hop from inn to inn across Vermont. Others will meander on a weeklong journey through the vineyards of California. A riverboat will be chartered on the Mississippi, with riders fanning out through the rural South during the day and rejoining the paddlewheeler for a gourmet supper and a night's sleep as the ship heads downriver. A bevy of tandems will wend their way between castles and chateaux along France's Loire Valley, while another group forces its way over the high cols of the Pyrenees, retracing the great climbs of the Tour de France.

The majority of riders will find their own way, carry their own gear, and set their own pace. Some will be on guided trips, with lodging, meals, and routes already designated. Some will be camping; others will be staying in posh resorts. Some will be riding for the sheer pleasure of the trip; others will be raising money for a variety of worthy causes.

Why do we tour on a bike? Well, it's fun. An airplane allows you only a partial glimpse of the land below, and in a car or a bus you're isolated behind glass. A bike moves at about the right speed to really experience the country you pass through. You are open, vulnerable, exposed to the world around you.

Once, on entering an Oregon coast campground, we were met by a man carrying two steaming cups of coffee. "We've seen you over the last couple of days and thought we could trade some coffee for some stories about your ride."

In France an elderly lady waved us to her side of the street and invited us to view the stunning walled village wrapped around the river below her immaculate gardens. Napoleon had slept in that house on his way to be crowned emperor by the Pope.

On a tandem in the hills of northern Italy, we were surprised to hear someone say, "You have a lot of water bottles." The speaker was a trim, balding rider in his mid-sixties easily spinning up the grade. It turned out he was a former Olympian, a sprint racer forty years ago. He redrew our day's route to create a beautiful and stimulating ride through a rich historic landscape.

It looked like the perfect French countryside restaurant, with massive, rain-darkened stone walls and tiny window panes over flower-bedazzled boxes. But one look at the linen tablecloths and formal attire of the diners convinced us to ride on. They didn't need a pair of wet and muddy cyclists. Just then the owner came out, telling us that *oui,* they had a table we could have and it was not too late for a meal. We apologized, pointing out our wet clothes and the tandem we had leaned against the wall. "No, no, it is all fine, we have room for the *velo* in the back, in the courtyard." Under an awning we found a place for the bike, and we were given a pair of towels to complete a brisk wash. Inside, at the table to which we were guided, the petite chairs with upholstered seats were discretely covered with towels. Our protests were met with a dismissive flip of a hand, "It is not a difficulty. You are cyclists." And the four-course lunch that followed was a meal to remember.

Why do people tour on a bike? You meet the people whose homeland you are visiting. A bike and jersey are an ice-breaking introduction anywhere you wander. People who would never think of stopping a passing car for a conversation feel totally free to share a word or a coffee with you. If you hesitantly ask for directions, don't be surprised if the person draws in two or three friends to help you create a special route.

Cycle touring opens your eyes to the vast span of our world, from a bird call to the ripples of wind playing across a grain field. It offers great satisfaction for a hill crested, exquisite excitement at the end of a downhill glide, delight at the vista opening up around the next corner. You relearn that a clear day is a gift, that rain is often welcome, and that wind can be a learning experience. Water tastes better, and you have a secret delight in earning the calories you consume after a day of riding.

Best of all, cycle touring is easy. Virtually anyone can do it safely and comfortably. So come ride through these pages, and you'll gather the basic gear and skills needed to take to the road. Whether you're a man or woman, child or senior citizen, a few days on your bike will reinvigorate you and restore your pleasure in the world.

CHAPTER ONE

The World of Bicycle Touring

They wobbled into the campground at the end of the day, dehydrated, hungry, and so sore they could barely dismount from their bikes. And yet they wanted very much to enjoy their first attempt at bicycle touring.

They had started with the best of intentions. They had chosen a route through beautiful scenery over uncrowded roads marked with hills steep enough to be a challenge yet low enough to be an achievable goal. They set out to cover a moderate number of miles each day. And they had good bikes with gearing adequate for the terrain, although not what most cyclo-tourists might choose.

Yet here they were, slumped to the ground, red-faced, and almost panting. We handed them a bottle of carbohydrate-rich energy drink and started boiling water for pasta. Even if they gathered the energy to cook, it wouldn't be for a while, and they needed to eat now.

What was going wrong on their ride?

They weren't carrying water bottles and didn't know how much liquid and how many calories they needed for a day in the saddle. Their bikes weren't adjusted for them—saddles too low, handlebars too high, and shoes that put the arches of their feet over the pedals. They were exerting a lot of energy, but most of it was wasted before it got to their rear wheels.

They looked to be in the highest gear as they plodded into the campground, a sure clue that they had missed the basic truth of cycling: Pedal quickly in a midrange gear, and you'll cover more ground with less energy than someone pedaling in a high gear with a slow pedal rate. This also gave them sore arms from tightly gripping their handlebars, the cause of their headaches. Their positions on the bikes created sore backs and painful bottoms.

As they wolfed their spaghetti, we passed along tips and techniques we had learned through painful experience and from other riders—energy foods, hydration, ways to identify upcoming hazards and pass safely through them. We tried hard not to play the grizzled veterans of the road, because if there is anything we have learned through the years, it is how little we know.

They fiddled with their bikes that night, making a few small adjustments, and the next morning they rode away. I don't know if they quit and shipped their bikes home or happily finished their planned ride. We never saw them again. We discussed, as we rode along, how much more comfortable our first tours would have been with access to information about basic bicycle touring skills. You'll find all of those skills detailed in the chapters that follow.

APPROACHES TO TOURING

Rest assured, there's a touring style out there that'll fit you perfectly:

Fully Supported. You just ride and let a touring company take care of everything else. They arrange where you're going to sleep, make dinner reservations, supply lunch and snacks on the road, move luggage, draw maps for each day's route, and have a mechanic in a van close at hand to patch your flats and carry your luggage. Depending on the service selected, you may be staying in historic inns each night or camping in tents. Fully supported tours are on the pricey side, but the pampering is sometimes worth it.

Events. You join a group, usually a large one, riding a mapped route. Most of these include budget camping, meals, and road support, and your gear is carried from one campground to the next. And most events raise money for good causes. If you want to have a great time riding for a good cause, you can choose one spanning a weekend or one going coast to coast.

Fixed Base. Settle into comfortable quarters in the heart of the area you want to explore and venture out each morning on a day trip to take in the sights. You ride a featherweight bike, and a shower and familiar bed await you each evening. And you can book in as many lazy days off the bike as you choose. Like the fully supported ride, you might have a guide and a support van/sag wagon along. Or you might be on your own.

Credit Card. Stick a change of clothes and a credit card in your oversized seat bag and head off down the road. Stay in motels or inns, eat in local cafes.

You'll have to plan ahead, though, to make sure you're not miles from anywhere as darkness falls. You also won't have the security of a support van and mechanic if things go awry.

Self-Contained. You're on your own. You cram forty pounds or so of clothes and camping gear into your panniers (bags mounted to luggage racks) or bike trailer, select your own route, set your own speed, plan and prepare your own meals. This is freedom on two wheels! It's the most work, both to plan and to pedal, but it's also the most economical. You can change your mind and route on a whim, dawdling around attractions and pounding out the miles when the mood strikes you. The format of the ride is only part of the picture. One tour may concentrate on racking up a lot of high-speed miles each day, or do just 10 to 20 miles, with long breaks at restaurants and museums. Another may challenge your hill-climbing abilities or focus on improving bike-handling skills. Yet another may offer a gender-specific group raising money for a specific charity. Be frank with yourself about the format you'd like to ride with, and the effort you want to, or can, expend.

Figure 1-1. Think of your bike's panniers as rooms in your house and pack accordingly. Pack kitchen items in one; a tool kit, spare food, and first aid kit in another; a tent and sleeping bag in one rear pannier; and clean clothes in the other. Store dirty clothes in a bag on the rear rack and maps, documents, camera, and sunscreen on the handlebar.

TOURING ON YOUR OWN

On a nonsupported tour, you choose the route, the time, the food, the lodging, and you provide the mechanic to keep your bike running perfectly. What you might not suspect is that the total cost, the real cost, of a nonsupported tour is pretty darned close to that of a supported tour of the same level of comfort and adventure if you figure in the value of your own time in all the planning, scheduling, and logistics. Tour operators are able to buy in quantity, which gives them an edge in feeding a group, arranging lodging, and prorating group needs over an entire season.

If, however, you share our passion for details and delights along the way, planning a trip is nearly as much fun as riding it. Chambers of commerce, state departments of transportation, and state tourism departments are good sources for maps and bike routes. Adventure Cycling (P.O. Box 8308, Missoula, MT 59807; (800) 721–8719, www.adventurecycling.org), which started by mapping out the Bicentennial Bike Route across the country, has expanded to become a giant warehouse of North American bike maps and guidebooks. Spend the few bucks necessary to join their organization, even if just to support bike touring.

Heading overseas? Look at the vast resources of the Cyclists' Touring Club (69 Meadrow, Godalming, Surrey, Great Britain, GU7 3HS; 0870 8730060, www.ctc.org.uk, or cycling@ctc.org.uk). It has around 70,000 members and a huge supply of maps and route information.

If you used good sense and joined a local bike club when you first started riding, you will have first-hand information at your fingertips. Where did your friends ride, and what did they find? Check for guidebooks in your local library, on the Web, and at bookstores and cycle shops.

If you choose to go self-contained, you pack clothing, house, bedroom, and kitchen on your bike. Well, make that your tent, sleeping bag, camp stove, and pots. You can set up a home away from home anywhere, within reason, if the spirit moves you. We've carried our bikes a few feet into the woods and out of sight on the Oregon coast when miscalculating our speed to the next campground, and we've also set up our tent between the sauna and the swimming pool, right across from the espresso stand, at a private resort. Many, but certainly not all, public parks with campgrounds charge a reduced fee for hikers and bikers. You'll meet people with a shared interest and often garner tips on road conditions and sights along the way.

The downside? Our basic camping outfit for two weighs about twenty pounds. Add food, and we each roll along with ten to fifteen pounds of extra weight. With clothing, cameras, personal items, and bike gear, we're carrying forty pounds each. Many of the campgrounds we found have showers (good), but few have washing machines (not good). Also, you may not be comfortable camping among a group of strangers, and comfortable or not, you'll need to secure your bike and possessions each night.

When we're touring self-contained, we try to budget for a motel every third or fourth night: comfy beds, a tub for soaking, a place to lock up the bike, and a chance to let someone else do the cooking. Most motels have washers and dryers, as well.

Of course, the ultimate camping outfit weighs less than an ounce. The credit card is a boon to cyclists. Leave most of your camping gear at home and ride from inn to inn. We did that for a month across southern France, and the convenience—and the luxury of a dry room after a drizzly day—was splendid.

The downside? A motel room each night costs significantly more than pitching a tent. Planning is vital to avoid being left on a long and empty stretch of road as the sun goes down. If you're cycling through a popular vacation area, you may have to make reservations, eliminating some of the spontaneity of the ride. A motel room also isolates you from the local people and other cyclists. B&Bs offer up social time as well as a place in which to secure your bike.

Support yourself! Find a half-dozen like-minded cyclists and vacation together. Five of you can ride, and the sixth can drive the van with all your gear. Trade driving duties each day or each half day. You can camp or motel it, you can ride with unloaded bikes, and a tired cyclist can always hitch a ride in your personal sag wagon.

The downside? Finding a group of cyclists willing and able to vacation at the same time in the same place can be difficult, although the costs, split half a dozen ways, aren't too bad. If you're starting somewhat close to home, you can use your own support vehicle, but vacation destinations far afield require a rental. Keeping track of five riders is often a challenge as well. The van driver can hand out snacks and water bottles and collect or distribute clothes as needed, but this job can be boring.

SOLO OR WITH FRIENDS

If you ride solo, you're also the mechanic, route-finder, and cheering section. You are the sole source of gumption on the ride, with no companion to boost your spirits. You'll have to carry all the spares, tools, and gear, too. It is exhilarating yet lonely. You become vulnerable to the play of your emotions. Your senses are heightened and you have no one to stabilize your ups and downs or to help evaluate your experiences. There is some hazard in traveling alone, but it's no greater than in most other activities. I don't recommend telling strangers you are riding alone, and you should probably be vague if pressed about where you're camping or staying. Carry a cell phone for emergencies.

Riding with one or more companions, on the other hand, is an exercise in compromise. You have to agree on the level of comfort, the route, miles per day, and speed. You must work out what to eat, and when, and learn to forgive each other's quirks and habits.

Five or six riders make a good-sized group. The group usually splits into two or three riders on the road, few enough not to impede motor traffic yet allowing someone with whom to share the joys and work. It also means each subgroup can carry one spare tire and a set of bike tools rather than loading every rider down with spares and tools.

Everybody should have a map of the day's route, with rest or food stops to regroup. They can be a pain to make but a delight to have and use. Cell phones are pretty darned handy too. Unfortunately, they don't work everywhere. Small radios have limited range (2-plus miles), eat batteries, and add weight. A map and a schedule are always useful.

GUIDED TOURS

You can improve your chances of having a great riding vacation with a bike-tour company by doing your homework. Start by thoroughly assessing your own wants and needs. Do you want catered meals, snacks delivered from the sag wagon as you ride, and a soft bed in an upscale B&B? Would you prefer a buffet breakfast, brown-bag lunches, and a tent? Will you panic riding in a group or when someone hands you a map after breakfast with a route you must follow to the day's destination? Do you like 100-mile days or 25-mile days? How many days do you have for your ride, and where do you want to go? Unless you're a super-fit ultradistance rider, you're not going to cross the country in a two-week vacation. When can you ride? Vermont leaves don't turn scarlet in July, and high mountain passes tend to get snowed in by January.

The level of luxury on a fully-supported tour establishes the price. Gourmet food, luxury resorts, and bottled water in the sag wagon may run $400 per person, per day. Basic motels, good food, and slightly larger groups per guide and/or sag wagon may cost $200 per day. An event ride for charity, with meals served under canvas and nights spent in your own tent, may cost $100 to $150 per day. You put up your tent, and they truck it to the next night's stop.

Adventure Cycling, Cyclists' Touring Club, and the back pages of *Bicycling* magazine are great resources when you start to search for tour operators. When you've found a handful of operators offering tours where and when you'd like and within your budget, start prying. How long have the companies been around? An established company could be jaded, while a start-up may exceed your dreams in an effort to establish itself; but a company that has survived for a few years has proven it can cope with some of the challenges that invariably crop up. Ask for a list of previous customers and call one or two to inquire about their experiences. And find out how experienced the guides and support people are.

What happens to your deposit if you have to cancel? Can you change tours and dates with little penalty? If the operator has to change the itinerary or dates, what are your options? Some of us have no vacation flexibility. Do you have dietary restrictions? If so, can the operator accommodate your special needs? On many tours, you'll be on your own for certain meals—perhaps a lunch during a rest day at a resort or a dinner in a larger community known for its restaurants.

If you're riding a bike with unusual tires or a different chain, be sure to alert the operator and bring your own spares. Same goes for spokes and brake pads. Don't spring a surprise on the tour mechanic. What's the ratio of support vans to riders? One van for six riders is luxurious but pricey; one for fifty or sixty is woefully inadequate. Some tours are aimed at a particular type of bike, such as tandems, while others cater to retired folks, gearheads who hammer the whole ride, or families with young kids.

"Beginner," "recreational," and "advanced" are relative terms, so ask for an itinerary and elevation profiles. For a tandem team, 50 flat miles is typically a couple-hours ride, but add in 10,000 feet of climbing, and 50 miles turns into a long day of low-gear effort. Explain your own riding abilities and fitness. Are the guides simply there to get you safely down the road, or are they going to share with you the history and nature of the land you pass through?

Last, remember to bring a supply of good humor and optimism. This is your vacation, so make up your mind to enjoy it, despite an occasional rain shower or other inconvenience.

CHAPTER TWO

Your Bike and Your Body

THE TOURING BIKE

The best bike for touring is sometimes the one that's available. Many years ago, Thomas Stevens rode from Oakland, California, to Boston, Massachusetts, in a brisk 104 days. He rode 3,400 miles on an "ordinary," one of those bikes with a huge front wheel and no gears, averaging 1.36 miles per hour. He faced a few disadvantages on that 1884 ride—there was no road network, no maps, and often no bridges. He had such a good time that he continued on east, crossing Europe and Asia before relaxing on a steamship from Japan back to the Bay Area. He rode around 13,500 total miles.

That said, most bicycle tourists choose the traditional diamond-frame, drop-handlebar road bike. It works well and is light, sturdy, reliable, and relatively inexpensive, and parts (including tires) are readily available. Hybrids sport a similar frame but with a flat handlebar like a mountain bike. The flat handlebar has fewer positions for your hands and doesn't give you the same aerodynamic advantages. Mountain bikes, if their off-road knobby tires are swapped for high-pressure slicks, ride like a very sturdy hybrid. They tend to have lower gears, which work to your advantage. All three types can be boxed and shipped via air or rail, albeit at a hefty price.

FITTING YOUR BIKE TO YOU

A properly fitting bike won't make you ride faster or go farther, but it will allow you to ride as easily, efficiently, and comfortably as possible.

Many bike shops cater to young, fit, and skinny late-adolescent males. Racers, if you will. They are often unwilling or unable to cope with folks outside that narrow band. If such a shop won't spend the time to find you the proper fit and accessories, politely leave and find one that will.. Too many women have been intimidated onto bikes that aren't at all suitable, and too many men have been placed atop bikes that don't work for their age or desires. On the other hand, there are some really great folks out there that will go well beyond all reason to find the bike that works best for you. Hey, you deserve excellence. Don't accept less.

Step one is to measure yourself in inches. Stand with your back against a wall and your feet a comfortable 6 inches or so apart, then place a large hard-back book between your legs. The spine should touch your crotch, with the adjacent side firmly against the wall. Have a friend measure the distance from the ground to the top of the book. That's your inseam. Next, measure from the top of the book to the small "V" at the top of your sternum. That's your torso

Figure 2-1. Hand position on a drop handlebar roadbike

length. Now hold a pencil in your closed fist with your arm stretched out horizontally ahead of you and measure from the little boney bump at the outside edge of your shoulder to the pencil. That's your reach. Finally, measure the span from the little bump on one shoulder to the corresponding bump on the other.

Let's play with the numbers. Stand over a bike you like with your feet flat on the floor. If the bike has a horizontal top tube, you should have about 2 inches of clearance. Many bikes now have a top tube that slopes down from the head tube to the seat tube, a design quirk. If your chosen bike has a sloping top tube, just imagine a line coming back horizontally from the top-tube/head-tube joint.

Add your torso length and reach, then divide this number by 2 and subtract 6 inches. That's pretty close to the top-tube length you want. Think of two people that each have a 29-inch inseam. If that was the only important measurement, they would fit comfortably on the same bike. But say one of them has a long torso and the other a short torso. Oddly enough, that's one of the differences between men and women. The man might fit comfortably on our imaginary bike, while the woman would have to stretch uncomfortably just to reach the handlebars. Good bike builders understand this, which is why bikes are made with differing length top tubes.

What if you find a frame that is almost perfect, even to the paint job, but the top tube is marginally too long? Look at the same bike model one size smaller. The top tube will be proportionately shorter, and you can adjust the seat post (the rod connecting saddle to frame) for the correct height.

Remember measuring across your shoulders? That's a good width for your handlebars. Typical road-bike drop bars are as narrow as 38cm or as wide as 44cm. Too narrow a bar will constrict your breathing; too wide will put excessive weight on your hands (numbness) and allow your spine to slump from your shoulders (back pain).

Wheel your bike onto a level surface. Adjust the saddle fore and aft until the clamp is at about the midpoint of the saddle rails. Now place a carpenter's level on the saddle, nose to rear edge, and adjust the saddle angle until it's as level as possible.

Now multiply the inseam length you measured earlier by .88. Rotate your pedals so that the crankarms are right in line with your seat tube. Slide your saddle and seat post up or down within the seat tube until the distance between the top of the lower pedal and the top of your seat matches your answer.

You should be wearing your cycling shorts and shoes for the next step. Roll your bike over to a doorway and mount up. (You can use a trainer, but you'll have to shim the front wheel until the bike is level.) Hold the sides of the doorjamb for balance. Put your heels on the pedals and rotate the cranks backwards. Your legs should be fully extended at the bottom of each stroke with little bend in your knee, and your hips should remain level through the stroke. If your hips are rocking back and forth to keep your heels on the pedals, the saddle is too high. Fiddle with the height until your knees and hips toe the mark. Once you own the bike, mark this height on the seat post for future reference. When you put the ball of your foot over the pedal spindle (or axle), you'll have the perfect bend in your knee. Put some miles in, and if the saddle feels off, adjust it up or down a minuscule amount.

Most of us ride happily with level saddles. If you convince yourself that you'll be more comfortable with the nose sloping down, you're slipping toward a sore ride. You're also slipping forward on the saddle itself, building pressure on your arms, hands, and knees, which is a prescription for pain. You'll kink your neck squinting out from under your helmet rim, leading to a headache. And you're not going to relieve any pressure on your personals. If a level saddle proves uncomfortable after plenty of test miles, you might experiment by tilting it less than 3 degrees. Male riders are more likely to tilt the nose up, female cyclists down.

You need a helper for the next step. While on your bike in the doorway or next to a wall, balance yourself and rotate the cranks until they are horizontal. Have your helper hold the string of a plumb bob (any weight on the end of a string) on the front of the bony bump just below your kneecap of your leading foot. The weight should be dead center over the pedal spindle under the ball of your foot. If it isn't, adjust your saddle forward or backward until it is.

Really tall folks that like to ride long distances with a slightly lower cadence might prefer the plumb bob to hit about 1cm behind the midpoint of the spindle. Adjust that later if you wish, but start with your plumb bob over the pedal axle.

Off your bike and out of your cycling shoes for comfort, put a board or yardstick across the saddle and over the stem of the handlebars. Level it with your carpenter's level. Most road riders start with their bars about an inch below the level of their saddle. With experience, many riders lower their bars 3 inches or more. Recreational riders might start with the saddle and bars at the same height or with the bars down about an inch. At my age, fitness, and flexibility, I'm pretty comfortable with my bars about 2 inches below the saddle on my road bike and the tandems.

It might seem as if you'd be more comfortable with the bars higher than the saddle, as you wouldn't have to crane your neck to see ahead. But when you're leaning forward about 45 degrees, looking ahead is a breeze. If you raise the bars higher than the saddle, you shift your body weight over the rear of the bike and put more of it on the saddle. Every ripple or bump in the road sends your spine thumping into your brain. Lowering the bars shifts your weight forward, some on your hands and more on your legs. Your knees and elbows work like shock absorbers, saving your body and reducing the jarring on your bike.

The final adjustment is not easily made but is key to a comfortable ride: the reach, or distance, from your saddle to your handlebars. If the reach is too great, you're going to roll your pelvis forward as you grasp the bars. This takes your weight off your sit bones and mashes the tender tissues in front of that area onto the unforgiving nose of your saddle. Pain in your personals occurs not because the saddle is too hard, but rather because you are trying to reach too far. Bars that are too far away or too close can also cause hand, lower back, shoulder, and neck pains.

One quick way to identify an improper reach is to watch a tired rider on an ill-fitting bike. He or she will continually scoot forward or backward on the saddle. If your reach is too long, you'll want to slide forward on the saddle. This

Figure 2-2. Front axle obscured

moves your sit bones off the wider part of the saddle and puts tender flesh on the saddle horn.

Let's check your reach. Put your now mostly adjusted bike on a trainer and make it level. While wearing your cycling clothes, get on your bike and spin the pedals until your upper body is loose and relaxed. Your back should be a comfortable 45 degrees or so, and your elbows should be slightly bent. Look ahead down the road. Rest your hands on your brake hoods. Have your helper drop a plumb bob from the tip of your nose. An imaginary line is OK but not as accurate. The plumb line should fall about an inch behind the center of your handlebars. For a rough guide, look down at your handlebar and front axle. Your front wheel axle should be out of sight behind the handlebars (figure 2-2). The only adjustment option if you already own the bike is a trip to your local bike shop for a new stem. Stem lengths range from 6 to 14cm.

So you're miles from anywhere and you just lost or broke a cleat. You can't keep your foot on the pedal and you have no other way home. A miserable but possible fix is to wrap a few turns of tape around your shoe and pedal, being very careful not to restrict your pedal rotation. You'll need a friend to do this for you. Just remember, you won't be able to unclick and put your foot down on that side, so it's also a prescription for falling over.

The cleats on the bottom of your cycling shoes are part of your bike, whether or not you think of them that way. You can adjust your foot position over the pedal and the angle of your foot and the pedal. Fore and aft is easy. The ball of your foot should be directly over the pedal axle. If you pedal with the arch of your foot over the pedal spindle, you lose the power of the big muscles of your legs. You also lose a big part of your legs' ability to help pump blood through your arteries. If your feet are positioned so that the pedal spindle is between the ball of the foot and the toes, your Achilles tendons will ache and your legs will cramp. And you'll probably think about bagging cycling.

Many of the pedal/cleat combinations sold today allow for a fair amount of "float." This means you can twist your feet back and forth slightly while still clicked into the pedal. It makes for a more comfortable ride. Some hold your foot in a predetermined position, and some are adjustable. A broad rule of thumb is to draw an imaginary line bisecting the sole of your shoe with your cleat at a right angle to that line. Your foot should be in a natural, comfortable position on the pedal. Now go for some very easy miles in this position, and be considerate of your knees. If you are uncomfortable, stressed, or strained, adjust the angle. After five hours or so, check your pedals and cleats to make sure everything is still tight. Once you've worked out the ideal cleat position, scribe a fine line around the cleat or trace a line around each cleat with an indelible marker to make it easy to reposition a loose cleat or replace a worn one.

Some folks still prefer riding with toe clips and straps. They work, but consider: Your foot will be locked into one position by the cleat hooking on the pedal and the toestrap holding your foot and cleat to the pedal. You have no "float" to relieve pressure on your knees. You must reach down and release the tension on your toestrap in order to free your foot. Forget, as I once did, and you'll topple over like a tortoise on its back. For comfort, convenience, and safety, learn to ride with clip-in pedals.

LET YOUR BODY FINE-TUNE YOUR FIT

Cycling comfortably involves adjusting your bike to fit your body. It isn't the other way around. Learn to listen to your body. If you're not comfortable, something doesn't fit. And if something doesn't fit, you're wasting energy that could be better used to ride on down the road. For example, if the big muscles in your upper leg hurt and have no energy, the answer is in your fingertips. Shift into a larger rear cog and spin along comfortably. It doesn't matter if Lance Armstrong can spin that gear; your legs are saying you can't.

Maybe you have a headache and painful shoulders and neck. Ride without your gloves for a while. Your knuckles look like white-topped mountains erupting from your hands, and your forearms are as rigid as marble. You're clutching so hard you've created a tension headache. Relax, bend your elbows, and let your forearms wobble like jelly. Enjoy the view.

A similar headache occurs if you forget to drink or eat. A lack of fluid will also lead to painful muscle cramps. Your body is chastising you for ignoring your basic needs. Squinting into sun glare can also create a pounding headache. Wear sunglasses and take care of your eyes.

If your lower back hurts, most likely your stem or saddle is positioned wrong. If your hips wobble side to side when you're pedaling, your saddle is too high. Lower it a bit. If your hips don't wobble, odds are your stem is too low. Raise it slightly. The stem should be marked to show the maximum amount you can raise it out of the steering tube. Don't exceed that amount. If your lower back still twinges, swap your stem for a slightly shorter one.

Stem height can trigger other responses from your body. A low stem, which forces your head way back in order to see, triggers a sore or stiff neck. If your hands pain you, you have too much weight on them. Raise your stem, and the weight will go back on your feet. Your knees have a few things to say, also.

If the front of your knee hurts, you're straining to overcome a low saddle. If the back of your knee is sore, you're likely overextending your joint due to a tall saddle.

If your Achilles tendon hurts, it's because your cleat is too far forward and your toes are pressing down on the pedal. Move the cleat forward until the ball of your foot is over the pedal axle and you'll be fine. And if your rear end is sore or numb, not from overexercise on your first excursion but throughout the ride, you likely have too much weight on your seat. Lower your stem slightly and then check your saddle height. You may want to lower your saddle a quarter inch or so.

What if you have the squirms, shifting back and forth on your saddle? If you're on a tandem, your first problem is surviving because your partner will be seriously considering murder. Every time one teammate shifts the other gets jarred. If you seek comfort by sliding forward, the nose of your saddle may be pointed down. Level it. Or your saddle may be pushed back too far; adjust it fore and aft on its rails. If you're still edging forward, your stem is probably overly long.

Perhaps you push back during the ride. The front of the saddle may be angled slightly upward. Level it. Or the saddle may be pushed way ahead on the clamps at the top of the seat post. If so, adjust the fore and aft position of the saddle. Or your stem might be too short, so you're shoehorned into place. You may have to replace the stem, or just maybe you can make do by lowering it a bit. Lowering your stem increases its apparent length; raising it shortens the length.

Most road-bike bars are flat from the stem out to where the bar turns forward and down to the brake hooks. You may be able to find a bar that comes slightly higher from the stem outwards.

TRICKING OUT YOUR BIKE

So we now know that for a touring bike to work well it has to be the right size. It also has to be a middle-of-the-road design, meaning a midweight bike. Super-lightweight bikes are costly and fragile. Heavyweights wallow along and are no fun to ride. We don't need—although we desire, perhaps—top-of-the-racer-line components such as Shimano's Dura-Ace or Campagnolo's Super Record. By stepping down a level, we can get great performance with a friendlier price tag. But I don't recommend dropping all the way down to bottom-end components that will wear out or break all too soon. In the bike industry quality and price do go hand in hand.

The closer to vertical the seat tube is on your bike, the more maneuverable and "twitchier" the bike becomes. A more angled frame is more stable and comfortable. If you measure the chainstays on a number of bikes, from the bottom bracket to the slot that secures the rear axle, you'll discover a range of sizes. Short stays help shape a compact and maneuverable bike. Long stays stretch out the overall length and create a bike that wants to glide in a straight line. Long stays also mean you'll have more room over the rear wheel so you can hang panniers off your rear rack without banging your heels into them on each stroke.

Look on the front forks and on the seat stays (the tubing from the rear axle up to where the seat tube and top tube join). Down near where the axles fit in, you should find small threaded eyelets, two on each side of each wheel (figure 2-3). One set of eyelets secures the lower supports of your luggage racks (front and back), and the other supports the struts for your fenders. Go-fast kids like the look of fenderless bikes, but after your first ride in the rain you'll love fenders.

Figure 2-3. Two rack screw eyelets mount both rack and fenders.

On the seat tube and on the down tube you should find matched pairs of threaded holes. That's where the cages that hold your water bottles are mounted. Next, look at the crank arms. You want three chainrings on the front—medium-large, medium-small, and tiny (figure 2-4). That's half your gearing system.

Figure 2-4. Triple chainrings give you more gear combinations.

WHAT DO YOUR GEAR NUMBERS MEAN?

Most cyclists refer to their gears in one of two ways. The first is as a fraction, as in, "I'm spinning a 42/21." This means the chain is engaged with a 42-tooth chainring in front and a 21-tooth in the rear cassette. The other method gives you a handy way to compare one chainring/rear cog combination with another. For instance, a cyclist may say she's riding a 72-inch gear, which means one revolution of her pedals moves her bike the same distance as one revolution of a wheel that is 72 inches in diameter. Think about the historical photos you've seen of bikes with giant front wheels.

To figure out any gear combination, divide the number of teeth on the chainring in front by the number of teeth on the cog in the back, and then multiply by 27. Most bike wheels used to have a 27-inch diameter, even though today there are more 700mm wheels than the slightly larger 27-inchers. The size of the tire on the wheel also affects the true, rather than relative, measurement. To make it simple, if you have a 27-inch or 700mm wheel, use 27 inches. If you have 26-inch wheels, use 26, and so on.

Why all this gearhead figuring? Because your bicycle gears don't progress in ten steps on the smallest chainring followed by ten on the middle and ten on the big ring. You will hop from one chainring to another as you find the gear that works for the conditions through which you ride.

Figure 2-5. Rear limiting screws keep the arm from shifting the chain beyond the largest or smallest cog and off the bike.

You also have eight, nine, or ten cogs mounted as a cassette on your rear wheel (figure 2-5). You choose a gear by derailing your chain from one ring to another and from one cog to another. That's what *derailleur* means.

A racer wants gears that are very close together so she can fine-tune the effort she's putting out to stay at speed. She'll spin her pedals at 90 rpm or so, and use the gear combinations to keep her speed as fast as possible at that cadence.

A tourist needs a wider choice of gears, to allow her to maintain an efficient 80- to 90-rpm pedal cadence without straining knees or exhausting legs. If her lowest gear is around 20 inches—a 24-tooth chainring and a 32-tooth rear cog with 700mm wheels—she can twid-dle up a 6- to 7-percent grade in the mountains for half a day. She might be doing only 4 to 5 miles per hour while expending the same amount of energy as if she were going 20 miles per hour on the flats, upwards of 800 calories per hour. A 100-inch gear (a 50-tooth front chainring and a 14-tooth rear cog) gives her a speed of about 25 miles per hour at a pedal cadence of 80 rpm. That's the two ends of the spectrum. The challenge is to come up with cassette cogs and chainrings that will provide a smooth jump from one combo to the next—each gear being 10 to 12 percent different than the next—along with a rear derailleur that can accommodate that large a difference. If I had a choice, I'd opt for a 20- to 24-inch low gear and be satisfied with the largest gear that my derailleur could handle.

I've evolved from shifters mounted on the downtube to shifters mounted on the end of my handlebars to an integrated brake-and-shift-lever package. Technology is great! The integrated system provides crisp, accurate shifting while letting my hands rest near the brake levers.

Pedals that lock to your shoes with cleats are much more efficient and keep

Figure 2-6. Recessed cleat

Figure 2-7. Pedal for recessed cleat

Figure 2-8. Protruding cleat

Figure 2-9. Pedal for protruding cleat

your feet from accidentally falling off the pedal. When your shoe and pedal function as a unit, you dramatically increase the power you apply without increasing effort. By twisting your heel a few degrees you can release your shoe from the pedal to put your foot down when stopping.

There are two families of pedals and cleats. On one, the cleat is recessed into the shoe sole and the pedal hooks into the cleat (figures 2-6, 2-7). On the other, a cleat protrudes from the shoe sole and this clips into the pedal (figures 2-8, 2-9). They are both very good, with one huge mechanical difference. If the cleat is recessed within the sole, you can walk without marring a floor, clicking and clattering, or sliding. I tour with recessed cleats. There are numerous man- ufacturers of pedals, cleats, and shoes. Just make sure that the shoe you like is compatible with your favorite pedals.

Let's assume your bike has 700mm, 26- or 27-inch wheels. Choose alu- minum alloy rims, because they are strong and provide a good braking surface. Look for wheels with thirty-six spokes in a three-cross pattern. This means each spoke crosses three others between the hub and the rim. This is a con- servative wheel, and you can find good wheels with as few as sixteen spokes.

Spoking patterns range from radial—straight out from the hub to the rim without crossing another spoke—to cross-four.

A three-cross, thirty-six-spoke wheel is strong and resilient, and when you break a spoke, as everyone does eventually, it'll likely hold its shape until you get to a friendly bike shop. Highly stressed wheels, with few spokes and fewer crosses, are likely to flop into a taco shape if you break a spoke. You are going to have more weight and more air resistance with this wheel than with a high-tech competitive racer disk. If you are really light, you may get by with a thirty-two-spoke wheel. Or you could choose a thirty-two-spoke front wheel (less stress up there) and a thirty-six-spoke rear.

If you weigh 250 pounds or more, call Co-Motion Cycles in Eugene, Oregon, and ask about their Mazama. It's a single, hybrid-style bike built with tandem components and materials. It is pricey—you won't get much change from a $3,000 bill—as are most custom or semi-custom bikes, but it comes with tandem wheels, which means forty-two to forty-eight spokes.

For most of us, quick-release axles on the wheels are great. The quick release holds the axle, and thus the wheel, on your bike. It is a rod with a nut on one end and a lever-and-cam on the other, fitted through a hollow axle. Close the lever firmly and the gadget clamps on both dropouts. Most quick-release levers are marked "open" and "closed" or may be slightly cupped. When the curve of the bend sticks out, the lever is closed; when it faces the bike and the end of the lever points out, the lever is open (figures 2-10, 2-11).

Figure 2-10. Quick release lever—closed

Figure 2-11. Quick release lever—open

Most bikes have wheel-retention tabs, little fingers or a ridge that stick out near the mouth of the axle dropout. They are designed to keep a slightly loose wheel from falling out of the dropout and bike. To remove a wheel, open the quick release and then unscrew the nut on the non-lever end until the wheel comes free.

To reinstall a wheel, center it between the frame, or fork, and tighten the quick-release nut clockwise until you feel resistance when attempting to close the lever. You should be able to push the lever fully closed, but the lever should leave an impression in the palm of your hand. If you can't close the lever, you've tightened the nut too much. Make darned sure the inside faces of the quick release are up against the flat side of the dropout and not hung up on one of the wheel-retention tabs. That misaligned wheel *will* come loose.

Most cyclists position the quick-release levers on the left side of the bike. That's important in the rear so the lever won't interfere with the derailleur, and it's just a convention in the front. Many riders align the lever with a stay or fork blade where it's unlikely to snag anything.

There's nothing wrong with axle nuts that clamp your wheel to the frame. They are a little slower than quick releases when changing a flat, but they are quite secure as long as you firmly tighten them in place. The only disadvantage I see is that you must have a wrench for those nuts. We have axle nuts on the rear of both our tandems and quick releases on our single bikes.

Racks are held in place by bolts placed through the bottom eyelets of the rack struts and into threaded eyelets by the dropouts. Bolts can work loose on bumpy roads, and you can secure them in three ways: smear the threads with a locking compound such as Lok-Tite; tighten a locking nut on the protruding threads inside the eyelets; or drill a small hole through the part of the bolt that extends past the threaded eyelet and twist a small piece of wire through it.

You have two choices for packing your gear: a trailer or panniers. A trailer obviously holds more, but this can lead you into carrying way more stuff than you need. Trailers also weigh more than the average set of panniers. I suspect that the total cost of a trailer and its associated packing bags is greater than the total for racks and panniers. On the other hand, panniers hang more weight on your bike, its rear wheel, and spokes than does a trailer. Front and rear bags also affect bike handling, perhaps more than a trailer. Braking with either is probably a wash, as you have to slow the same amount of weight.

Panniers should be sturdy, waterproof bags that mount on your front and rear luggage racks. Balance the weight fore and aft and left to right. The ritual is to find waterproof panniers, test them, and then wrap anything that has to stay dry in plastic anyway. By the way, you don't want wimpy racks when all your possessions are dangling from them. Pack the same way if you're towing a trailer.

If you choose to tour with a child, from a toddler to age six or seven, you have only one real option: The kid should ride within the protective envelope of a trailer. Seat belt, shoulder belts, and a helmet are absolute necessities.

Mount a speedometer, or more properly a cyclocomputer, on the handlebars. Your speed isn't all that important, but you need a reasonably accurate mileage counter to position yourself on the day's map. Also, mount fenders. You'll appreciate them on the first damp day, and the rider following you will really appreciate not being washed down. And add a chain protector to your drive-side chainstay to keep your chain from gouging and battering the chainstay. It's mostly cosmetic.

Figure 2-12. Antipuncture tire liner

Get a quality tire pump with a pressure gauge and a flexible hose connecting the pump body and valve. The pump must work with the type of tube valve you have—Presta or Schrader—and it should create more air pressure than your tire needs. If your tires require 100 psi (pounds per square inch), the pump should be capable of supplying more than that with plenty of strokes. If your pump only delivers 65 psi, you'll be wobbling on squishy tires, and you'll soon wreck them.

Use biggish, high-pressure tires, 75 psi or more. That means 1 1/4- to 1 3/8-inch tires on a 27-inch wheel or 28 to 38mm tires on 700mm wheels. Kevlar tires protect against some flats, as do antipuncture strips inside the tire. You'll still get some flats, but not

Figure 2-13. Cable lock

as many. Never pump up your tires at a service station. Their massive air pumps can't be controlled precisely enough to keep from blowing the tires right off the rim.

Last, buy a good lightweight lock. A determined thief with time can rip away any lock, but you should get one that will slow down the bad guys and save your steed from opportunistic snatch-and-run thieves. Also, record your bike's serial number, and make sure your homeowner's or renter's insurance carries a full replacement clause in the event of theft.

THE SADDLE

Put on your cycling shorts and head outside, not to your bike but to the nearest curb. With your legs comfortably bent, sit down on the curb. Most of your weight is now on your ischial tuberosities, the sit bones at the bottom of your pelvis, and here on the curb you're discovering how the support should feel. When you sit in your saddle, you should feel that same level of support. Use the narrowest saddle you can find that offers that support. Wider saddles will chafe your thighs and can even splay your legs out. If the saddle is too narrow and you don't feel the desired support, the nose of the saddle will push up against your soft tissues and make your ride miserable.

Your saddle should be lightly padded. A deeply padded saddle, even at the proper width, may let your sit bones sink in to the point that the saddle rubs you the wrong way. The "anatomical" saddles with a groove or an actual cutout along the top are quite comfortable for some riders and incomprehensible for others. Variations have been around since the late 1800s. Proponents believe the cutouts reduce potential numbness, bruising, and yeast infections, as well as reducing erectile dysfunctions. Some riders never have any of these difficulties, no matter what saddle shape they ride. The important thing is to find what works for you.

A noseless saddle might seem like a great idea—and it is on a bike mounted on a trainer. On the road, however, most cyclists control their steering and balance by pressing their thighs against the saddle.

Some seat posts hold the saddle clamp in place with a single vertical bolt through the body to the post and into a moveable clamp pressing down on the saddle rails. Others have a pair of nuts on a threaded rod extending side to side at the lower edge of the saddle cover. Both can hold a saddle in the proper position, but the single vertical bolt makes your saddle position much easier to adjust.

CHAPTER THREE

What to Wear

DRESSING THE PART

Cycling gearheads who delight in tech talk debate cog sizes and stem lengths, as if metal defines comfort when you're rolling out the miles. But for most of us, fabric defines the pleasure of our ride.

Let's start from the bottom up. This is where you meet the bike saddle, a vital pressure point for the five or six hours your're actually putting the bike down the road. The most comfortable cycling shorts are made of six, or better yet eight, separate panels, shaped with a stretchy fabric to create a skin-tight, nonbinding garment. The back should be relatively high to keep the shorts from pulling down when you're bent over the handlebars. A smooth and seamless or flat-seamed "chamois," once leather but now usually a synthetic pad treated with an antibacterial, forms a cushioning and sweat-absorbent crotch. The lower leg hem lightly grips your upper leg to reduce friction and chafing. Some shorts have an elastic waistband, others built-in suspenders creating a bib. They're worn without underwear.

Traditionally, shorts are black, which doesn't show greasy hand marks from when you grabbed your chain or the smudges and guck you pick up along the road.

Some more modest folks prefer "baggies," classic cycling shorts attached within loose, long-legged shorts. Look for them in the mountain-bike clothing section. Many women choose a "skort," classic cycling shorts wrapped inside a short skirt. While several companies sew them, the only women I know that wear them have used Terry Bicycle garments. Team Estrogen is a Web-based retailer offering a wide range of female-specific clothing, including skorts.

Most shorts come to just above the knee to prevent your thighs from chafing against the saddle or top tube. Knickers have a slightly longer leg, covering your knees. If mornings are cool, this keeps your knee joints warm. If mornings are nippy, tights will cover you from ankle to waist. Think Lycra or Spandex pantyhose. Most tights don't have a chamois and are worn over shorts. Some tights, normally a heavier weight and with a windblock or rain-repellant front, do come with a chamois and are worn in lieu of shorts.

Leg warmers are a practical alternative to tights. They are just the legs from a pair of tights, and extend from your ankle up to and under the leg hem of your shorts. The elastic band of the hem holds the tights in place. Well-thought-out warmers have a zipper at the ankle, allowing you to remove them without taking off your shoe. They offer almost the warmth of tights in a package you can stuff into a jersey pocket for quick changes.

Top off your outfit with a bicycle jersey. Today's materials wick sweat away from your skin, stretch to allow a full range of unconstrained motion, and don't flap annoyingly in the wind. Most will have two or three pockets in the back. I have a couple of jerseys with zippered pockets, but most utilize an elastic top. I can stick a Gore-Tex jacket or vest in one pocket and a plastic bag of Fig Newtons in another and still have room for a plastic bag holding a few bucks, my ID, and a couple of individually packaged baby wipes.

The zipper at the neck should close snugly but be easy to open for venting off heat in a climb. I have a short zipper on my long-sleeved winter or cool-weather jersey, but I like a zipper that opens down to somewhere between my sternum and navel when riding in the heat.

Bright-colored jerseys are more than a fashion statement. Any edge you can give yourself in the visibility game is worth it. A club or team jersey is an introduction when touring in Europe, while copying the clothing from a pro team is, well—if you can't do the walk, don't do the talk. A club jersey marks you as a serious cyclist.

Jerseys seem long when you stand up, down to midbuttock or so in the back. They'll ride up a bit when you're on your bike but will still be long

Stick a light plastic garbage bag in your jersey pocket. One day you'll really heat up during a long, steep climb but will find the top of the hill cool and the fast descent on the other side darn cold. At the top, spread the bag open and slip it under the front of your jersey as a wind block. It can make a chilly descent tolerable. It's not a new idea. Racers back in the old days used to layer newspapers under the fronts of their jerseys during fast, cold descents.

enough to cover your back. Long sleeves versus short sleeves is a matter of preference. I'm always adjusting things to keep at a comfortable temperature, so I usually wear a short-sleeved jersey and carry arm warmers on a cool morning. Long sleeves don't give me that option. But in the winter or early spring, the long sleeves are nice.

A lightweight vest of Gore-Tex or similar breathable material is great for layering and will shed wind and light drizzle. It'll also fit in a jersey pocket for quick changes. A jacket of similar material is super for a cool morning or when caught in a drizzle. If it's pouring, and thus cool, I prefer a big, loose, long waterproof jacket with a snug neck, a long tail to keep spray off my back, and zippers under the arms for ventilation, such as the Burley bicycle rain jacket. Rain pants will keep you dry, but most cyclists I know prefer tights when caught in the rain.

Booties fit over your ankles and shoes, with a cutout on the bottom for your cleats. They won't keep you totally dry in a deluge or toasty in a frigid winter blast, but they will raise your comfort level. In a pinch, you can slip on plastic bread sacks or small grocery bags and seal the tops with rubber bands around the ankles.

You have two choices when it comes to shoes: road or mountain. Road shoes are light, have a rigid sole for maximum cycling efficiency, a very narrow heel to keep your foot away from the chain and to pare away weight, and are miserable for walking. Mountain bike shoes tend to be heavier, have slightly more flexible soles and wider heels for walking, and aren't as efficient in transmitting your energy to the pedal. While touring, I prefer a mountain bike shoe, although some riders find the very small surface of some pedals uncomfortable with the flexible sole. It can feel like stepping on a pebble, so put plenty of miles on your shoes and pedals before starting a long tour.

You wear fingerless cycling gloves for three darned good reasons. One, the cushioning and padding in the glove protects your palm and the nerves running between the ball of your thumb and the outside edge. You really don't want numb hands while riding. The padding also cushions your hands and arms from some of the road shock. Two, gloves protect your hands from wind and sun. Three, and hopefully you won't have to learn this, a glove will protect your fragile palm if you wreck. You can still ride with a palm gouged by road rash, but it's extremely uncomfortable.

Cycling gloves also give you distinctive tan lines—tan fingers and wrist and a tan oval on the pale back of your hand. It's the equivalent of a secret fraternity handshake and serves as an introduction to other avid cyclists. Long gloves with fingers are neat for cold-weather riding, but it's hard to find ones with comfortable padding. If you start riding in the chill morning and continue into the heat of the day, you'll need both long and fingerless gloves. Or pick up a pair of polypro liner gloves—about $10 or so—and wear them over your fingerless gloves. They are small and light, and you can stick them in a pocket when the temperature rises.

Sunglasses are vital. They should protect you from the sun and be impact resistant to guard against flying debris. They should be light and should fit under your helmet. Lenses should wrap around to give you side protection. If you wear expensive prescription glasses, consider safety glasses designed to fit over them. I wear contacts when I ride, not out of vanity, but for the protection offered by my sunglasses. Some sunglass and protective-eyewear makers offer prescription lenses in their sunglasses.

I wear dark, UV-blocking glasses during the day. Come evening or when riding under flat, gray light or in the wet, I switch to light yellow shooting glasses. Light yellow and pale orange glasses tend to increase contrast and provide a better picture of the road.

Some riders wear a sweatband in the heat and switch to skier-type ear-warmers when the temperature drops. Others wear a thin fleece skullcap when it's cool. Funky bike caps offer a wee bit of insulation as well as a tiny bill. You can also fit a fabric cover over your helmet to block the vents for a warmer and drier ride.

HELMETS

Your bicycle helmet should have a Consumer Products Safety Commission (CPSC) sticker showing that it meets safety standards. If your helmet is less than three years old and has an American Society for Testing and Materials or a Snell Foundation sticker, it meets CPSC standards.

A white helmet offers the best visibility, night or day, and it wouldn't hurt to add several swatches of reflective tape. It should be so darn comfortable that you wear it every time you're on a bike. A properly fitting helmet reduces the risk of serious head injury by 85 percent and brain injury by 88 percent.

Most helmets are called road, mountain, or sport helmets. That's just styling, though, as all offer the same protection. Way more important is fit. Your helmet should ride even and level on your head, with the front edge resting just above your eyebrows. It should be snug, but not aggressively so.

Helmets are typically made with a foam liner within a thin plastic shell and are designed to crumple in a wreck. They come in different sizes, with a collection of fitting pads and adjustable straps to fit your particular head size and shape. The better ones have an adjustable retention device at the back to fine-tune the fit. Vents direct air flow over your head, cooling you and carrying off heat. Almost any helmet is going to be cooler than riding bareheaded. Today's helmets are light. A good helmet might weigh only 10 to 12 ounces and will lighten your wallet by $30 to $80.

Test the fit by holding your helmet firmly in place, chin strap disconnected, and attempt to turn your head from side to side. Next, tip your head up and down. You should have less than an inch of movement each way. If the helmet moves enough to expose your forehead or cover your eyes, you need to adjust the straps or possibly change the fitting pads. If it flops around a lot, the helmet may just be too large. A loose helmet won't protect you in a wreck. and may even slip in front of your eyes when you ride over a rough patch. Wear your riding sunglasses when trying on a helmet. Check that the ear piece and frame are comfortable when the helmet is in place.

If you wreck, you probably should replace your helmet. The foam liner has been compacted as you bounce along. As a rule of thumb, figure the working life of a helmet is about four years. That's due to sun, sweat, pollution, and the aging of the components.

Figure 3-1. A properly positioned helmet

CHAPTER FOUR

Health and Nutrition

DRINK UP!

One of the main reasons you become grouchy when cycling is that you're not drinking enough water. Few of us have the discipline to drink the amount of water we need, on or off our bikes. We need to drink about eight 8-ounce glasses of water a day just to regulate our body temperature, lubricate our joints, and flush the wastes out of our body. Time on the bike increases that amount.

About an hour before you start, drink a 16-ounce bottle of a sports drink. Or drink a pint of water about two hours before the ride. For a different taste, try green tea, fruit juice, or vegetable juice. Avoid the caffeine in coffee or dark teas, which tends to increase urine production just as you're trying to fill your water reservoir.

Plain water works pretty well, but for a longer, harder ride in the heat, you might want a sports drink containing salt and other electrolytes. Learn which brands you like and can tolerate on your training rides before your tour. Your body needs time to acclimate to a new drink. Electrolytes, which include calcium, magnesium, sodium, and potassium, help maintain the balance of our bodily fluids and help regulate heart rhythm, muscle contraction, and brain function. You should be getting about 100mg of sodium per 8 ounces.

I use a pair of bottles: one with water and the other a sports drink. I more or less alternate between the two. I'll sometimes make a drink by adding about 1/4 teaspoon of salt to a quart of weak, lightly-sugared lemonade. I want it lemony, not sweet. Limes can be used for a different taste.

When you're on the bike, take a couple of big swallows every quarter hour. How much water you need will depend on the heat, humidity, and your level of exertion, but you'll be fine if you just drink about 20 to 28 ounces of water an hour. You'll know you're drinking adequately if you start looking seriously for an outhouse every couple of hours.

If you're analytical (or anal), weigh yourself just before you go on a fairly vigorous ride. Drink normally during the ride, but hit the scale before you drink anything upon returning home. The difference is the amount of water you weren't able to replace during the ride. You should slowly drink about 20 ounces of water for each pound you've lost.

SQUIRT DOWN THAT H_2O

Some riders avoid drinking because they don't like taking one hand off their handlebar and lifting a water bottle out of its cage. And they get nervous holding the bottle in front of their face. Beat that by holding the bottle at about nose level off to one side and squishing the soft sides of the bottle to squirt a drink in your mouth. Moving one hand to your handlebars near the stem will keep you from swerving as much while you reach down for the bottle.

Many riders swear by hydration packs, but I don't like carrying anything on my back, nor do I want to clean it every day.

Let's suppose today is a high overcast day, medium warm, low humidity, and with a bit of a tailwind. You might not feel the slightest bit thirsty but you're riding right into a potential case of dehydration. You probably won't even realize that your joints are starting to feel stiff and that your thought process is getting a bit muzzy. Signs to watch for include a dry mouth, sticky saliva, and no desire to stop at a restroom every couple of hours. If your urine is dark yellow and pungent when you do stop, you're becoming dehydrated. And if you're only making a few drops, you're slipping well out of balance.

Find some shade, put your feet up, and sip down a sports drink. Plan on sipping a couple of quarts of water over the next two to four hours. If you can, grab a seat in the sag wagon for a low-stress ride to camp. Some folks do well with a rehydration drink such as Pedialyte or Lytren. It's also a good idea to have a chat with your doctor before starting out on a strenuous multiday trip.

Learning to recognize the signs of dehydration, and the ways to prevent it, is a lot like carrying a spare tube. You or your riding buddies may never have a flat, but it's a helluva lot easier to be prepared.

RIDE TO EAT, EAT TO RIDE

Despite all the charts, rules, and instructions that float around the cycling community, there is no right way to fuel up for a good day on your bike. There are some bad ways, though, mostly involving junk food and inadequate consumption. The harder and longer you go, the more hills you climb, and the air temperature establish the amount of fuel you need.

If you and your buddies are going to hammer right from the get-go for 50 miles or so, take on a balanced load of protein, carbohydrates, and fat a couple of hours before you meet in the parking lot. At 6'1" and 185 pounds, and having reached a responsible age, I like a serving and a half of oatmeal cooked with raisins and doused with skim milk, a big glass of orange juice, a banana, and bread with cheese. Dates, figs, dried apricots—I like to pad the oatmeal with any fruit at hand. I'll finish it off with a couple of cups of real coffee (more addiction than benefit).

At 70 to 100 miles with a more gradual beginning, I'll go for a stack of pancakes, a couple of eggs, ham or sausage, a banana or citrus fruit, fruit juice, and real coffee. A blueberry muffin with the second cup of coffee goes down well. With a bigger breakfast and plenty of protein and fats, you'll start leisurely.

You might burn about 40 calories per mile on this ride, and it doesn't take long to start draining your fuel tank. If you want to hammer in the hills, you can burn off more than 60 calories per mile. Your digestive system is only going to process about 200 calories an hour, so keep it stoked. The faster you go, the more energy you'll need. You'll burn about 400 calories moving your bike 15 miles in one hour. Boost that to 20 mph and your energy needs go to almost 800 calories. Running out of fuel can turn the end of a fun ride into slogging misery.

Legendary cycling coach Eddie Borysewicz liked cracker-and-very-lean-meat sandwiches in the early parts of a ride to keep protein levels up. He liked horse meat, but buffalo is pretty darned good, also. Peanut butter inside pita bread is easy to eat and to pack in a jersey pocket, as are alternate fillings such as a soft cheese or turkey and cream cheese. You won't get a sudden flush from these, but they keep a flow of energy heading to your muscles.

Midmorning is a great time to climb off the bike and grab a muffin or two. The same snack food you've been nibbling on all morning is good for lunch, which is also around the time you should switch to a more carb-intensive diet. Energy bars work for a lot of people. Find brands and flavors that get along with your stomach. I'm partial to fig bars, four of which add up to 200 calories.

They are also inexpensive, easy to pack in a plastic bag, and easy to eat. Bananas, at about 100 calories, meet the same criteria, even though you have a peel-disposal challenge. Dried apricots or prunes pack easily into a Ziploc bag and are easy to nibble while riding. Little new potatoes grilled with Cajun spices go down well and sparkle in your mouth, warm or cold. Commercial sports drinks can provide 200 calories and some of the nutrients you crave.

In the last hour of so of the ride, you won't digest most foods until you're off the bike, so I switch to an energy gel. I hate the consistency and dislike the packaging, which seems to be designed to promote littering, but the gels can boost you over the last humps. Candy bars give you a sharp spike of energy, followed by a steeper crash. Nutrients are sacrificed for sweet taste.

Your body is eager to sop up carbs and nutrients in the first hour after the ride. I'll usually swig down a bottle or more of water or a recovery-type drink and an energy bar. If you want to be a little more scientific, your muscles will take up glucose three times as fast in this postride window as they will six hours later. Sometimes a gooey cinnamon roll sounds better than anything else.

Supper is often pasta, a big salad, bread, a dessert (because I deserve it for riding that well), and a glass of wine. Given a choice, I'll have some kind of meat—skinless and boneless chicken or turkey—with the pasta for protein.

I don't go crazy precisely measuring out foods, calories, and percentages for a day of riding. Usually I just add a fourth meal. I do know that I work best with 40 to 70 grams of protein a day when I'm playing on my bike, and I try to eat about 600 grams of carbohydrates, somewhere in the range of 2,400 calories. Fats come in at around 15 to 20 grams. My friends and I typically take in about 70 to 75 percent carbs, 10 to 15 percent protein, and 10 to 15 percent fats.

If you are hungry or thirsty on a ride, you're already in deficit and you'll play catch-up all day. This can plague you the following day, too, because you've been breaking down your body for the fuel you should have been getting from food.

CHAPTER FIVE

On the Road

EASY, EFFICIENT RIDING

When pedaling at a walking pace along a paved path circling a park, you can ride as inefficiently as you want. But when you load 30 pounds on the bike, when you face mountains instead of molehills, and when the 50 miles you rode today are merely the prelude for another 60 miles tomorrow, you must hone your riding skills. Hey, we're riding for the fun of it, and when your riding becomes transparent and effortless, you can focus on enjoying yourself.

Let's get underway. Stand over the top tube of your bike. Apply your brakes so you don't roll. With your power foot, clip into your pedal or bring your toe under your pedal and rotate the crank backward until that pedal is at two o'clock—pointing ahead and about halfway between vertical and horizontal (figure 5-1). Release your brakes and simultaneously press down on the pedal. This starts your bike forward and lifts you up to your saddle. As your other pedal reaches the top of its revolution, place your foot on it and power ahead. Most cyclists like to clip in on the first revolution to give themselves the most control and the least chance for a shoe to slip from the pedal.

> If you left your bike out of your sight—locked, of course—before a ride, grab your handlebar at the stem with one hand and slightly lift your front wheel off the ground. With your other hand slap the top of your tire, as if you're trying to drive the wheel off your bike. You are. You're checking for a loose quick release or axle nut. Having a front wheel come loose while riding can ruin your whole day.

Figure 5-1. Pedal at two o'clock position

When you come up to a stop, first shift into a comfortable lower gear to make getting underway again easier. Put your weight on one pedal, at the bottom of the stroke, and shift your weight forward and off your saddle. Twist your other foot to release your cleat, lean your bike very slightly to the free side, and as you stop, put that foot down on the ground. Leave your other foot clipped in, and rotate the crank until that pedal is up at the two o'clock position.

Start with whichever pedal you like. Most cyclists stand on the left of their bike and clip in, their right pedal (by the chainring). That's probably because equestrians mounted that way, and we're just following along.

Why all the emphasis on just getting going? On the bike path it didn't make any difference, but with your bike loaded with all your gear, you need immediate control and power when starting up a slope on a narrow roadway. Some cyclists insist on sitting on their saddle with both feet firmly on the ground before they start. This forces your saddle too low, wrecks pedaling efficiency, and wipes out the power of your first pedal stroke from the two o'clock position. Your body weight adds power to your initial drive.

> Notice that greasy black "tattoo" of your chainring smeared on your calf? You twisted your heel inward and pressed your flesh against the chain or chainring, most likely when starting or stopping. Avoid the tattoo by learning to keep your foot straight when starting or stopping. You could as easily choose to mount from the right side.

Another common fault is to bring your clipped-in foot to the bottom of the pedal stroke and then push your free foot off the ground much like you did as a kid on a scooter. No power, no control. A few riders stand to the left of their bike, put their left foot on the pedal next to them, throw themselves forward, and swing their leg over their bike. This may have worked for cowboys in B-grade westerns, but that was with a horse and not a bike.

We're up and moving! Get comfortable, with your hands on the tops of the handlebars or over the brake hoods. If you are on the tops, your thumbs should be hooked under the bars so they won't slide off if you hit a bump (figure 5-2). If on the hoods, your thumbs should be on the other side from your index fingers (figure 5-3).

Without thinking, you've probably shifted your chain onto the largest chainring and the smallest cog in back and are laboring along. Your legs will

Figure 5-2. Hands on top

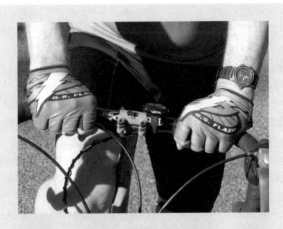

Figure 5-3. Hands on hoods

soon be exhausted, even though you're barely plodding along. Try shifting into the middle chainring if a triple, or the smaller if you have a double, and the middle cog in the back. Your legs will be moving much faster, and while this seems counterintuitive, you soon find that your legs remain fresh and strong. Sixty revolutions per minute may seem fast, but most touring cyclists are comfortable with a pedal cadence of 80 rpm, and fit racers might pedal at 100 to 120 rpm.

Think of having to put 100 pounds of flour on a high shelf. You can grunt and struggle and lift it in one bag, or you could easily lift it as ten 10-pound bags. It works the same on a bike. You can force the pedals around in a very big gear, fatiguing your leg muscles, or you can cover the same distance by shifting into a moderate, midrange gear and spin your pedals a number of times. Your legs won't fatigue, and your lungs and heart won't notice the extra demand after a little practice.

Some cyclocomputers will display your pedaling cadence. One way to learn the feel and joy of a high pedal cadence is to ride as a stoker on the back of a tandem driven by a skilled captain, as most tandems have a timing chain that keeps both sets of cranks revolving at the same rpm.

Your brakes are going to work when your bike is loaded, but you're going to have more mass to slow down, and that means a longer distance covered before you can come to a stop. Apply equal pressure on front and rear brakes, and slide backwards on your saddle. This will keep your weight better distributed over your wheels. If you really clamp down on your brakes, your inertia will tend to drive you forward, unweighting your rear wheel and reducing its grip on the road. If you lock your rear wheel, your bike will fishtail. If you lock your front wheel, you'll yield up most of your directional control.

There are three ways of guiding your bike around a corner. One guides you smoothly and precisely, one brings you around on the line you choose, and the third is really good for falling down. The last of these comes out of your past, when you rolled a tricycle up and down the sidewalk. You turned your handlebar in order to change direction, but this doesn't work on a bike. In fact, you steer with your other end, your posterior. You shift your weight slightly, the bike leans, and you turn. You apply sideways pressure on the long front saddle horn with your thighs to institute and control a turn. Think about that every time you consider a hornless saddle.

To glide around the corner on the line you want, push your outside pedal to the bottom as you approach and lean to the inside. You can bring your nose over your inside brake hood, and some riders drop their inside knee until it points to the ground. This all brings your body closer to the top tube, effectively lowering your center of gravity.

The most accurate way to go around a corner, and the one that gives you the most flexibility in correcting the path you're riding, is called countersteering. As you approach the corner, bring your hands down to the drops of your handlebar and slide your weight to the rear of the saddle. Put the outside pedal down at the bottom of its arc, and shift as much of your weight as possible onto that pedal. You are lowering your center of gravity and making your bike more stable. Keep your elbows bent. Your body is stretching out, long and low, along your top tube to spread your weight along the wheelbase.

As you begin the turn, push your inside leg against the bike's top tube. Don't stick your knee out. As you push your leg against the top tube, your hips will turn toward the outside of the turn. Your bike will dive rapidly into the corner yet remain completely under your control.

Press your outside leg's inner thigh against the saddle, pushing the bike down and to the inside in opposition to the pressure of your weighted outside foot. While you're doing this, gently pull on the handlebar with your outside hand. Riders once believed you should push down on your inside hand, but pulling on the outside creates the same effect while taking weight off your handlebar and increasing your control. Your body remains more or less upright, but your bike can lean as much as you need while carving an arc through the corner.

What if you slightly misgauge your path and are heading toward a mound of gravel or a wet spot? Relax your outside hand and ease off on the pulling. Your bike will rise up and make the arc of your turn broader. Once you're clear of the obstruction, increase your outside hand's pull to lean your bike over again and sail safely through the turn.

Teaching your muscles a new way to turn isn't a snap. Head for a level and vacant parking lot. Space out a number of paper or foam cups in a long line, leaving plenty of space between them. Swoop back and forth through the cups like a slalom racer, concentrating on leg pressure, lean, and pull rather than speed. Once you start feeling how the linked turns should work, move the cups closer together. The closer the cups, the quicker you'll have to turn.

To go through a corner quickly—that is, without braking off all the speed you worked so hard to achieve—is challenging unless you know just how quickly your brakes can slow you if needed. Find a nice empty road and mark the spot where you want to stop. Then lay out markers at 25 and 50 yards or so. Head back up the road a ways, then ride toward your mark at a brisk 20 miles per hour.

Start by applying your front and rear brakes equally. As you decelerate, your weight is going to shift forward. To keep from rotating tail over tincup over your handlebar, slide back on the saddle as you brake. The more pressure on your brakes, the farther back and lower down you should be. It is bad form, and downright uncomfortable, to slide rearwards right off the saddle and down on your whirling rear wheel. It's also harder, make that darn near impossible, to rise off that painful seat and regain your saddle.

How close did you come to stopping on your mark? Before braking, you covered 29 feet, 4 inches each second. Knowing how quickly you can reduce speed lets you hold your speed as long as possible and carry more speed out the other side.

What happens if you enter a corner too fast to negotiate it? If you lock up your brakes in a corner, you'll lose control, skid, and fall down. If you do nothing, you'll carom off the road. Your best bet—slowing down first would have been better, of course—is to jam your outside foot down with all the weight on it you can muster, lean your bike over as far as possible to drive the tires into the pavement, and carve as tight a corner as you can. Relax—if you can—every muscle and keep your hands on the drops. Your bike will turn better than you think, and you'll probably come out of the corner shaken but upright. If your wheels do come unstuck, you'll have a shorter fall to the ground and will slide rather than crash. This doesn't sound like a good thing, but it puts you in the best position to avoid nasty injuries.

> Riding down a bumpy road is a pain in the rear. Literally. Shift your rear derailleur over a couple of cogs to a larger gear, one that seems harder to spin. Without thinking about it you'll put more weight on your pedals to power your spin, and that results in less weight on your saddle. If you've not being thwacked by your saddle as hard, the ride seems more comfortable. Remember to keep your elbows bent and relaxed to absorb as much road shock as possible.

TOURING SAFELY

Bicycle touring is as safe a pastime as you can imagine—contemplative, reflective, and filled with all the time you need to enjoy the countryside. To slightly misquote Pogo and Walt Kelly, though, sometimes we meet the enemy and he is us. We share the road with cars, and that means we have to know and follow a common set of laws and regulations. If we fail to pay attention to what we are doing or if we don't understand how to control our loaded bikes, we're rolling into possible trouble.

Look around. Keep a clear picture of the road ahead while you check out the space immediately beside you. Sneak regular peeks back. Chat with your riding companions. Drink enough water so that nature forces you off your bike every hour or two to stretch. When you're weary, it's awfully easy to stare at your rotating front tire. Instead, sit up and take a deep breath. Glance at your cyclometer if you really want to know your speed or the distance you've traveled, but those numbers aren't going to change very fast.

I know of cyclists who zoned out and rode in a perfectly straight line right into the back of a parked bright yellow truck, and U.S. senators have been known to collide with parked cars. I've even seen folks ride slowly off the road into the bushes, totally unaware of what they were doing until far too late.

If you keep your wits about you, you won't have a speck of trouble. That said, you should be aware that hazards exist. Be aware of them, stand clear, and enjoy the day.

Edge of the Road

Be wary of the edge of an asphalt or blacktop road. For some reason construction crews like to lay down a nice broad base course when first constructing a road. But they sometimes don't apply a second layer quite as wide, and the third layer can be narrower yet. We're only talking an inch or so difference on each layer, yet the result is a steep stairstep from the road surface to the shoulder. If you absentmindedly ride off the edge, the jarring you take will clash your teeth together. There's a terrible inclination to turn back into the edge as you try to regain the road. Don't. Slow down and gauge a safe spot to climb back up. It is so easy to lose control on those narrow ledges and have your wheels kick sideways from underneath you. It hurts when it happens.

Many urban and suburban streets are built with an asphalt roadway butted up to a concrete curb and gutter. The joint between the two surfaces erodes and can form an irregular nasty rut, spreading out into the odd pothole. We all know we should ride on the right, as far over as safe and practicable. That doesn't mean bumping down the rough gutter. Ride on the right side of the lane, but stay on the roadway.

Storm drains that have a rectangular metal plate with long and narrow slots running parallel to the roadway are trouble. A wheel can fall into those slots,

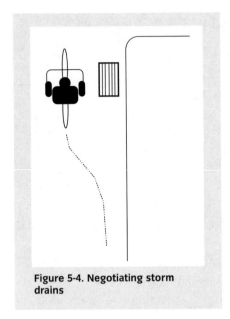

Figure 5-4. Negotiating storm drains

with painful and damaging results. Vertical drains cut into the face of the curb are often married to a deep indentation that channels water from the gutter sideways into the drain hole. Hitting that depression is almost as bad as a pothole, often with upsetting consequences. The safest drain for bikers is a metal plate with its slots cut at a right angle to the road surface. You'll roll easily over these, unless debris is sticking up. The safest bet is to ride slightly to the left of storm drains (figure 5-4).

Leaves are pretty on trees, but when they've flooded a gutter or mounded up in a corner, they're often slick. They can also conceal all sorts of nasties. Simply stay out of them.

Some rural roads conceal water bars—small ridges, maybe just an inch or so high, angling diagonally across a road on a hill. They channel draining water across the roadway like an aboveground culvert. As a hazard they are rare and small, but if unexpected they can toss you around.

Oil

Keep your eye peeled for oil. On dry pavement you'll see a light gray smear on the concrete. On asphalt oil will show as a long smooth dark streak. In the wet you'll see a shimmering multicolor wash faintly over the pavement. If you've been riding in the dry for a long spell and are then caught out in a sudden rain, oil that had soaked into the pavement will rise to the surface. In any case, avoid the oil if you can, because it's wicked slick. If you jam on the brakes or abruptly turn, you might find yourself in an uncontrolled skid. Braking distances can unexpectedly increase.

Riding through an oil patch on the straight is not a good idea. You're going to come to a corner, and oil on your tire tread is little better than oil on the ground when you lean for the turn. Ride loose; no sharp turns, no sudden acceleration, no abrupt stops. The only times I've ever had a problem with oil was in approaching an intersection—a wheel shimmying a bit on an oily build-up or a shoe with a projecting cleat starting to slide on a wet surface.

Bridges

Riding narrow roads in rural areas means crossing bridges with wooden decking. They're cute, but they're also slippery when wet or frosty. Slow down before you get to the bridge, and don't make any abrupt moves when conditions are questionable.

In most cases cyclists are shunted onto a narrow metal sidewalk that is often slick, debris-laden, and bumpy. The slipstream from passing vehicles will buffet you along the narrowed roadway. Some sidewalks are even interrupted by stairs. So you're on a narrow, cluttered path blasted by noise and wind—climbing when you start the bridge and on your brakes as you ease down the far side. Deliberately relax the knot in your shoulders, shift into a comfortable gear, and just twiddle across, minding your own business. If you're anxious, get off and walk. In fact, if you're crossing wet metal, definitely walk it.

Railroad Crossings

I like trains but hate rail crossings. They are slippery, rough, and inhabited by big things that go fast. And there is no easy way to ride around most rail crossings.

When you come to a rail crossing, slow down. There is a gap beside each rail and often broken pavement between the rails. Bang into this minefield and you can pinch your tube between tire and rim. That's a quick way of learning how to patch the twin holes of a snakebite flat. You can also pop some spokes (as I have) as well as ding a rim—even if you don't fall down.

Bring most of your weight off the saddle and onto your feet and arms. Your elbows and knees work like shock absorbers, and you'll take much of the impact off your bike. Be at right angles to the track when you cross over. Many times the rails cross the road diagonally, and if you ride straight along the road you face the horrid possibility of having your front wheel twisted out from underneath you as it passes over the rail and dips into the gap beyond. Creep up to the rails, and then turn to cross at a right angle at the last moment so that you don't swerve far out onto the roadway (figure 5-5).

Wet tracks are godawful! I once saw five tandems riding together all wreck on the same wet rail crossing with the rails slanting diagonally across the roadway. Slow down, get your weight off the saddle, ride straight and smooth, and don't panic—you'll be just fine.

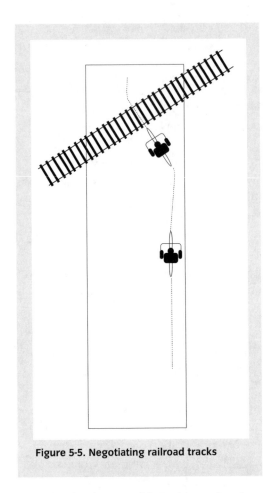

Cattle guards, more common in the West, have a dozen or so rails spaced closely together spanning the road at a right angle to keep cattle from crossing. Cross them slowly and you'll jounce around; cross them fast with your weight up and off your saddle, and you'll feel and hear a whirring from your tires. And cattle crossings always seem to be at the bottom of a steep dip. You brake on the descent as you scope one out, then sweat up the climb with no speed to help.

Paint

Lane markers between the roadway proper and the shoulder, crosswalks, even those big warning signs painted on the roadway itself pose a special hazard when you're on

Figure 5-5. Negotiating railroad tracks

two wheels. The paint fills in the road surface and creates a slick spot in dry weather and a potential skating rink during a drizzle. Newer paint is brighter than old paint and slicker. The easy solution is simply not to ride on the lines. If you are on a line, just ride easy without sharp braking until you can gently move onto real pavement.

Many roads today are marked with little flat reflectors along the lane and fog lines. Unexpectedly nudging one of these can be an eye-opener. They are easy to avoid and are unlikely to cause you to wreck, but you may still kiss the pavement if everything goes wrong.

Gravel

Gravel contains sharp rocks, it can slide out from under your tires in a turn, it increases your stopping distance when you're braking, and it can unexpectedly and sharply bog down your forward motion. You'll find gravel lurking on the outside of corners and where one road connects with another. Cars keep gravel off the roadway, but shoulders can be coated with the small rocks. Just be aware of where gravel accumulates and skirt the worst of it.

Blind Spot

Sitting high on conventional bikes gives us one great advantage—we can see over most cars as we watch for approaching hazards. That's also a great disadvantage, because we grow to rely on our vantage point, despite the fact that we can't see over oncoming trucks, buses, and motor homes. Lurking tight in

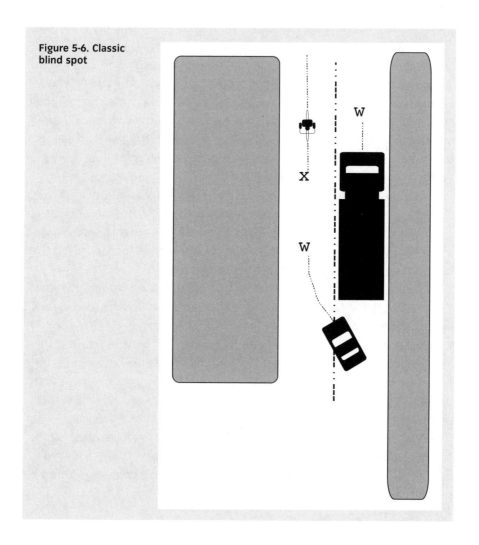

Figure 5-6. Classic blind spot

behind them, right in a moving blind spot, could be a car. Just as we can't see behind that bus, whatever is back there can't see us. If that vehicle pulls out to pass just as it comes to us, we're both in for a nasty shock (figure 5-6).

There's another blind spot, less obvious but just as hazardous. Hardly anyone driving a motor home knows how wide that vehicle is. Some drivers will pull clear to the other side of the road just to pass a bike, while others lumber right up the shoulder. I know of riders who have been clipped by mirrors or who bailed into the brush at the last second. An automobile driver, whether or not on a cell phone, can be just as inattentive to your presence.

BAD DOGS

Cyclists have met bears, deer, cattle, errant pheasants, and hungry raccoons, yet dogs usually top the cyclist's attack fears. Dogs own a chunk of real estate, and it's their bound duty to defend it from the likes of you and me.

So we're riding down the road and there's Bowser, just sitting in his yard. Bowser is probably going to wait until we roll past and then give chase. Option number one is to sprint, which obviously works a lot better if we're on the level or heading downhill. If Bowser is sort of loping along, barking with his ears and tail up, he is probably not too serious. If his ears are back and his teeth are glittering, it's time to stand up and fly.

If he charges up to you from in front, he's going to turn beside you. If he skids into your front wheel—it happens—you'll wreck. Sprint as he approaches and swing out into the traffic lane, if traffic permits, to give him a wide margin. Yell at him: "Stay!" or "No!" may make him hesitate long enough to let you ride off. Don't be quiet. Wake up folks a block or two away.

Heading uphill and worried about your sprint? Pop open the valve on your water bottle, aim, and squeeze. A sudden face full of water and a piercing yell will discourage most dogs.

What if you're trapped? Get off your bike and keep it between you and the dog. Yell for help. Hit 911 on your cell phone. If you're bitten, file a report with the local police with the location, a description of the dog, and the name and address of the owner if possible; and do it immediately. Get medical attention, and insist on proof of rabies vaccination, or have the dog quarantined.

Knock on wood, I've never been in a group seriously attacked by a dog. A few have given chase, but clearly it was all part of the game. Frankly, more cyclists have been annoyed by mosquitoes than by all the dogs we've rolled past on our rides.

SURVIVING A GROUP RIDE

Do you get nervous riding in a large group? Good! That's common sense. If you ride each day with the same few buddies, you'll soon learn to anticipate each rider's moves. But when riding with strangers, such as on a large tour, you don't know their riding styles and they don't know yours. The first rule in riding with a large group is to team up with a few—maybe four to six—riders and build a gap between you and the main body. You'll gravitate toward riders with similar interests and abilities, and you'll soon push each other to ride at a higher level. Magically, even a couple thousand bikes at a major riding event will quickly disperse into a whole passel of small groups during the day, flowing together at rest stops and lunch.

Riding in a large tour means constantly passing and being passed by other riders. Hold your line—ride straight at a constant speed—so faster riders can zip safely past. When you're about to pass another rider, first check that someone else isn't passing you. If clear, pull out to give a few feet of clearance and call out, "Passing on your left!" or a similar warning. Don't pass on the right, as this forces the other rider toward the middle of the traffic lane without warning.

We all like to ride side by side and gossip. That's legal in most states, but side-by-side riders take up a lot of road and make it difficult for a car to pass. When the roadway narrows, traffic increases, or your visibility is obstructed, pull into a single line. Yell out, "Car back!" when traffic approaches from the rear to let your group squeeze safely over to the right.

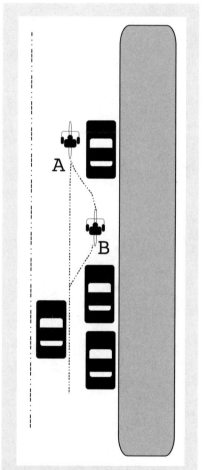

Figure 5-7. Be predictable and ride in a straight line—like Rider A—or signal your intentions. Do not dodge in and out of traffic like Rider B.

Some riders like mirrors mounted on their handlebars, some like a mirror on their helmet or glasses frame, and some will even mount a tiny mirror on the inside of their sunglasses. A mirror is great for confirming that a vehicle is approaching, but don't rely on it solely.

Lane changes or turns can be a hazard in our follow-the-leader world. The cyclist ahead of you may be perfectly safe in changing lanes for a left turn, but

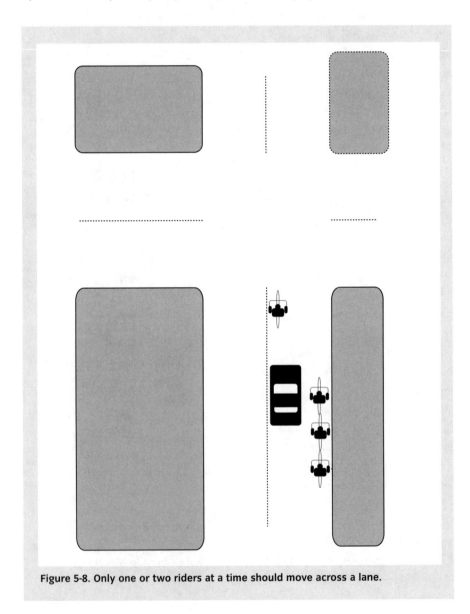

Figure 5-8. Only one or two riders at a time should move across a lane.

you *must* check back to make sure you have time and space to follow suit. Most groups do best by staying on the right side of a lane and letting one rider at a time scoot over to the left side for an upcoming turn (figure 5-8). If your group angles across in a body you can inadvertently block the road (figure 5-9).

Before you pull from one lane to another or make a turn, and after you've sneaked a peek to the rear, your should signal. Many kids learned that a left-

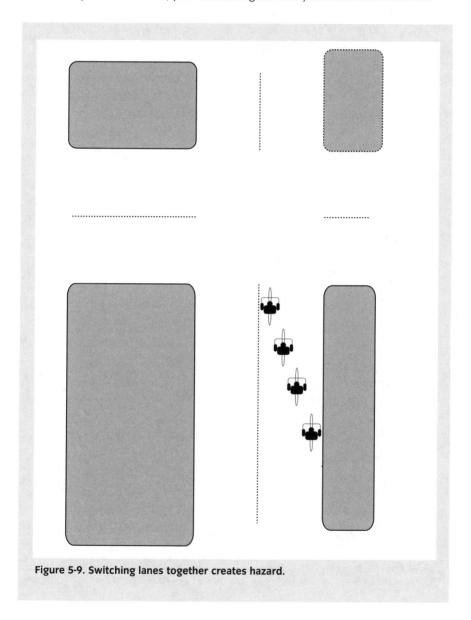

Figure 5-9. Switching lanes together creates hazard.

turn signal is done with your left arm straight out and a right-turn signal with your left upper arm horizontal and forearm pointing up. This makes sense if you're in a car, signaling from an open window. For bikers, it's better to just point in the direction you plan on going—with your left arm for a left turn and your right arm for a right. You won't confuse anyone with your intentions. While stopping, hang your left hand straight down, palm to the rear. Cyclists also use one other signal—they'll point at road hazards such as a pothole, broken glass, or a spray of gravel. The rider following you can't see the road just ahead, so offer a warning of trouble, if you can.

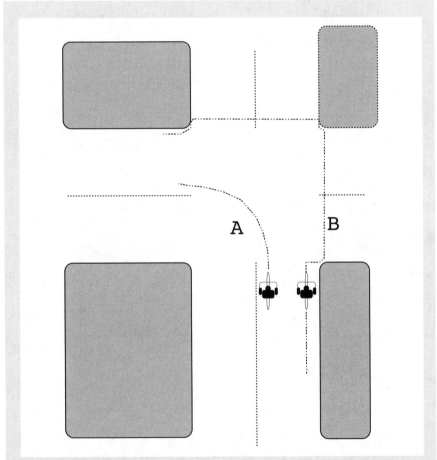

Figure 5-10. In less-congested traffic, you can make a safe left turn like Rider A. In heavy traffic, dismount and walk your bike across the street like Rider B.

You'll sometimes see cycling teams moving as a coordinated and disciplined body across a lane, with the lead and sweep riders serving as lookouts. What you don't see is the hours and hundreds of miles of practice that makes this teamwork possible. Don't emulate them unless you've ridden with them for all those miles.

Stay in a compact straight line while waiting at an intersection. A mob of cyclists piled up jams traffic something fierce. And it sounds obvious, but get off the roadway when you stop your bike, whether to read your map, change clothing, or wait for a buddy. Too many of us forget to just move over.

Watch for and identify the inexperienced or unskilled riders in your group: They wobble back and forth, they can't ride in a straight line, they're clutching their handlebars with a death grip, their arms are bar-straight and rigid from shoulder to hand, and they alternate between mashing their brakes and their pedals. Avoid these riders like the plague. They are the ones who will swerve in front of you, unexpectedly stop in the road, or wham into you from the side. Your best bet is to pick up the pace and pass them. If for some reason you can't leave them behind, create the biggest pillow of space possible.

If the group doesn't spread out, work your way to the front. That's easier to say than to accomplish, but it's well worth it. Lines of recreational-level cyclists tend to "accordion." The front riders maintain an even pace, but those behind tend to surge ahead and then slow down. In the back third of the group, it becomes a case of sprint and brake, which is exhausting and nerve-wracking. And most wrecks occur in the last half of a group, partly for the reason just given. You'll also find most of the unskilled riders dragging along in the back, adding to the challenges.

Beware of hills. More to the point, beware of riders who haven't learned the art of sitting down, shifting down, and twiddling up hills. Watch a cyclist with more power than skill start up a hill. Invariably, he will stand abruptly, which causes him to slow appreciably—if only for a second. A rider following close behind can thump into his rear wheel and wreck, often bringing down a number of other cyclists. Let the gap between you and the rider just ahead open up a bit when you start a climb, or ride a foot or so to the side.

With a little practice you can learn to rise smoothly out of the saddle, pulling your bike forward as you rise. Don't lunge forward, because this pushes your bike backwards. Some riders click into the next larger gear just before rising. This helps prevent mashing down on the pedal as your body weight comes on it, eliminating the lunge. Your pedal cadence will also be slower when you're standing on the pedals. When easing back into the saddle, push your bike forward to keep your speed steady. You can shift down to a comfortable gear after sitting down.

Practice riding with elbows bent, wrists straight, and arms and shoulders relaxed. If your arms are tense and your elbows straight, any slight bump on your arm will send the bike swerving. Bent elbows and relaxed arms work just like shock absorbers, smoothing out the road and preventing a minor collision from becoming a ground-scraping disaster. When relaxed, you can feel your forearms jiggle; when tense, you can see rigid muscles in your forearms. If you ride tense, your shoulders will knot up and you'll build a major headache. Ride loose and you can go farther and faster in greater comfort while working far less.

A BASIC TOOL KIT

When your bike breaks during a tour, you have one of two choices: fix it or rely on someone else to rescue you. About 99 percent of the time you can cobble together roadside repairs that will allow you to pedal on home or to a bike shop—if, of course, you've taken the time to learn the basics of bike repair and maintenance before you leave on that next long ride. Many bike shops offer clinics on this subject, or you can pick up tips from veteran riders or consult the myriad books on the subject. And don't forget to check all major components at the end of each day's ride on extended trips, which can head off a potentially dangerous situation on the road the next day, or at least help you avoid annoying delays.

What tools do you really need? First, good sense. Repairs and maintenance are easier to do at home, so get your bike in great shape before you head out on the road. Second, think about where you're riding. If you're crossing the back end of nowhere, you better be able to cope with any problem. If you're exploring a major city, you're probably close to a bike shop and all sorts of help.

The heart of my tool kit is a bike tool. There are a bunch of good ones out there, from simple to massive. I have a Park Tool, with the most common Allen wrenches, 8mm and 10mm wrenches, and assorted screwdriver blades. It also contains a spoke wrench, plastic tire irons, and a chain tool that works with the chains on my bike. There are several kinds of chains, and the tools aren't universal. I also have a couple of quick-repair links, which can patch a broken chain without tools. I have a combination headset/pedal/wheel axle nut wrench, and taped to this are an assortment of odd Allen wrenches for quirky tweaks I've done to my bike. Last is a small multipurpose tool, a SOG Pocket

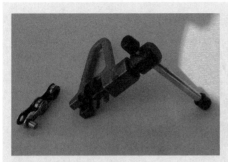

Figure 5-11. Chain tool

Figure 5-12. A quick and easy way to repair a broken chain is with a snap link.

PowerPlier, which gives me pliers, wire cutters, and a file—plus an assortment of screwdrivers and openers—in a 5.5-ounce package. Leatherman, Gerber, and Kershaw make similar ones.

On a long or isolated trip I might add a six-inch adjustable wrench and chain lubricant. I also have a small bottle of a general-purpose lubricant. Finishing it off is a small roll of stretchy black electrician's tape, which works for rim tape, seat repairs, handlebar tape, whatever. In my firstaid kit are a small flashlight and tweezers.

For parts, I carry a brake cable and a derailleur cable, both sized for the rear of the bike. A cable cutter would be nice, but I can shorten a cable with my multipurpose tool and then squeeze a cable-end sleeve to prevent fraying of the end. I carry spare spokes, too. I've seen folks carry a Kevlar cord gizmo that can be used as an emergency replacement spoke. I pack three or four nut-and-bolt combos sized for racks and/or fenders, and usually a spare water-bottle cage bolt in a plastic bag. On a longish ride I'll take a pair of brake pads, although I've never used them or loaned them to anyone else.

If you get a flat—and you surely will if you ride long enough—you should have a flat bag with the following items:

- A spare tube with the same valve as what's on your bike. A Schrader valve won't fit through a Presta valve hole, and the smaller Presta valve needs a rubber gasket adapter to fit in a Schrader hole. Two spare tubes are better.

Figure 5-14. Schrader valve

Figure 5-13. Tool kits should include the tools you need for your ride.

Figure 5-15. Presta valve

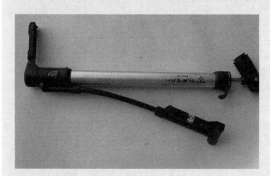

Figure 5-16. Frame pump

- Tire levers. Plastic is better than metal, and a screwdriver used as a substitute will gouge a hole in your tube every time.
- Patch kit. Use the kind with a tube of glue. These make a permanent patch.

- A boot. This is a 1-by-2-inch piece of tough cloth from a wrecked sewn-up tire or even a chunk of very thin tube. You put it between your tube and tire to cover over a cut in the tire. A gash through the tire body will flex and eat a hole in the tube.
- Wrench. If your bike has bolt-on wheels, you'll need a correctly-sized open-end box or socket wrench to loosen the axle nuts and remove the wheel.
- A pump. I use a short frame pump, small enough to tuck into a jersey pocket, with a fairly accurate gauge and a short rubber hose. It supplies 120 psi, and the rubber air hose means I can accidentally wobble the pump without ripping the valve stem out of the tube.
- I usually add a folding tire in case of terminal damage.

About the Author

Dennis Stuhaug started riding a bike with his first Columbia at seven years of age. He's a cyclo-tourist, a commuter, a competitive cyclist, and race official, as well as a writer for both popular and industry publications. He and his wife, Suzanne, have toured extensively, usually on a tandem, in North America and Europe.